Little
Hawaiian
Bento Box
Cookbook

Little
Hawaiian
Bento Box
Cookbook

Susan Yuen

MUTUAL PUBLISHING

Table of Contents

Rice 'N More

Recipes

Glossary

Foreword

Four years have passed since the publication of my first cookbook, *Hawai'i's Bento Box Cookbook*. During that period of time, God blessed me with so many wonderful opportunities to meet other bento enthusiasts, share new bento ideas on my blog, create more diverse bentos for a second book, *Hawai'i's Bento Box Cookbook: Second Course,* and most importantly, create more bentos for my children, Paige and Sean.

Little Hawaiian Bento Box Cookbook came about as a way to provide home cooks with a compact-sized collection of the most popular bentos and recipes from my first two cookbooks. It's the perfect size to travel with, keep tucked inside a kitchen drawer, or give as a gift to visiting family and friends who need ideas for making the perfect lunch for their kids.

Included is a chapter on sandwiches that require no cooking time at all and feature lovable bears, dogs, and butterflies—sure to entice even your pickiest lunchtime eater. There are local favorites: a variety of rice constructions, saimin, and musubi, as well as dishes such as Slow-Cooker Kālua Pork, Homemade Chicken Breast Nuggest, and Shrimp Tempura that allow you to not only create attractive bentos, but dinner for the entire family.

These are my children's favorite family recipes because they are the reason I began this bento adventure. My goal was to show my kids how much joy and love they brought into my life. They continue to inspire me to make bentos, and I love seeing their excited expressions and lovable grins when they unpack their bento lunches.

Important Tips

Decorations and Tools

- Regarding the use of picks and decorations, **never use with younger children as it could pose a choking hazard.**

- Color Mist™ is food coloring in an aerosol spray form and is made by Wilton. It can be found at Compleat Kitchen, The Executive Chef, and online at Amazon.com.

- For round cutters, look around to see what you have. For smaller circles, use straws or pastry bag tips. In craft or kitchen stores they sell fondant cutters of various sizes. Also look for round cutter sets.

Securing Food

- Very small pieces (1/4-inch) of uncooked angel hair pasta and somen can be used to secure certain moist foods as indicated in the recipes. The pasta or somen does become soft after 2 hours. **Do not use if your child will eat it right away.**

- Peanut butter, jelly, icing, or mayonnaise may be used to secure foods as well.

Packing food

- Choose the right sized container and fill the container such that the food doesn't shift around during travel.

- To prevent sweating make sure that all of the cooked food is cooled to room temperature before packing.

- For hot thermal containers, spend the money on a good reputable one. Preheat the thermal container with hot water and ensure the food is hot when putting it into the thermal container.

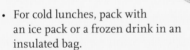

- For cold lunches, pack with an ice pack or a frozen drink in an insulated bag.

FLYING
FRIENDS

Bees
with Shrimp Tempura and Soba

Rice
Yellow Color Mist™
4 slices kamaboko
Nori for stripes and eyes
Shrimp Tempura (see page 70)
Soba (see page 77)

Form rice into oblong musubis (or use musubi mold). Spray with yellow Color Mist™. From the kamaboko, cut out small circles for the bees' eyes and cut out wings using a heart-shaped cutter. Cut thin strips of nori and place on the rice to form the bees' stripes. Arrange the kamaboko wings and eyes on the bees. Then finish the kamaboko eyes with small eyes cut out from the nori.

Ladybug Hamburger

1/4 pound of Hamburger recipe (see page 54)
Rice
5 slices kamaboko plus a cross slice of only the pink part for
   the spots
Nori for eyes
Carrot slice, blanched

Form hamburger into 1 large patty and 2 small patties. Cook
hamburger until cooked through. Place rice in the container
and arrange hamburgers.

With the kamaboko, cut 2 slices for the
mommy ladybug. Trim the ends (see
picture) and place on the hamburger. Cut
two small kamaboko circles to fit the two
small hamburger patties. Cut a small notch
so that it will look like wings, then place
on the hamburger. From the pink part of
the kamaboko, cut out spots for the ladybugs and arrange. Then cut out circles
from the white part of the kamaboko to
make the eyes. Finish the eyes with small
circles punched out from the nori and
placed on ladybugs.

Decorate the rice with small flowers cut from the carrot.

Dragonfly Saimin
with Slow Cooker Okinawan-Style Shoyu Pork

Saimin (Store-bought, prepared according to package directions. Keep broth in a separate thermal container.)
1 fried fish cake patty
4 slices fish sausage (or 1 slice bologna)
1 slice kamaboko
Nori, for dragonfly's eyes and stripes
Thinly sliced green onions
Black sesame seeds
Slow Cooker Okinawan-Style Shoyu Pork (see page 60)

---

1. Place saimin in a container. Cut the fried fish cake with a dragonfly-shaped cutter.

2. Cut two wings for the dragonfly from the fish sausage using a oval cutter, as pictured.

3. From the kamaboko, cut two circles for the eyes.

4. Finish dragonfly with nori eyes and stripes.

5. Place green onions on the saimin for the flower bed. Then cut two flowers from the fish sausage and decorate with black sesame seeds.

Chicken
with Imitation Crab Rolled Omelet

Rice
2 slices fish sau-
    sage (or 1 slice
    bologna)
1 strand of
    uncooked angel
    hair pasta
    (optional)
1 slice kamaboko
Yellow Color Mist™
Nori, for eyes
Decorative pick
Imitation Crab Rolled
    Omelet (see page 78)

Form rice into an oval shape. Cut two teardrop shaped wings
from the fish sausage for the chicken and secure with a small
pieces of pasta. If you don't want to use the pasta, prop the
wings on top of the chicken's body. Cut a circle out of the
kamaboko, then cut it in half and use one half for the beak.
Spray the beak yellow with the Color Mist™. Cut eyes from
nori and finish with a decorative pick for the chicken's comb.

FURRY
FRIENDS

Sheep Rice
with Pan-Fried Pork Chops

Rice
2 jumbo pitted olives
1 slice kamaboko
Nori for eyes
Pan-Fried Pork Chops
(see page 65)

1. Fill a silicone cup with rice.

2. Place one olive in the rice for the sheep's head.

3. Cover the top of the head with a little bit of rice. Cut two legs for the sheep from the other olive.

4. Then cut two circles form the kamaboko for the eyes. Then finish with nori circles.

Bear
Shrimp Fried Rice

Garlic Shrimp Fried Rice (see page 71)
4 slices of fish sausage
1 slice of the pink part of the kamaboko
1 slice of kamaboko
Nori for the eyes

Fill the two silicone cups with the shrimp fried rice. Take four of the shrimp and prop them up in the rice for the bear's ears. From the fish sausage cut four medium sized circles for the ears and two ovals for the muzzles. Cut out two smaller ovals for the noses from the pink part of the kamaboko. Then cut four small circles from the kamaboko for the eyes. Finish the eyes with small nori circles.

Mice
with Corned Beef Hash and Potato Macaroni Salad

Rice
1 hot dog, cooked
3 olives
2 slices kamaboko
Nori
1 slice cheddar cheese
Corned Beef Hash
(see page 58)
Potato Macaroni
Salad (see page 79)

Place rice in the container. Cut 6 slices from the hot dog for the mice's ears, and 3 small circles for their noses. Cut three olives in half and use the bottom halves as the heads. Cut 6 small circles from the kamaboko for the eyes. Then punch out eyes from the nori and place on the kamaboko. Arrange the mice on the rice. Then cut three cheese wedges from the cheddar and punch small holes in the cheese.

Mandoo Mice

3 Fried Mandoo (see page 62)
1 slice bologna
1 slice cheddar cheese
3 slices kamaboko
Nori for eyes
Celery for tails

1. Place the mandoo in the container.

2. Cut out 3 large circles for the ears from the bologna.

3. From the cheese, cut out 3 teardrop shapes (with the pointed tip cut off) for the inner ears.

   Also cut a cheese-shaped piece. With the cheese-shaped piece, take a small circle cutter and punch out holes and place it on the rice.

   Cut 3 circles from the kamaboko for the eyes. Arrange the ears and eyes on the mice. To finish the eyes, cut circles from the nori and punch out the inside of the circle, then place nori eyes on the kamaboko.

4. Cut thin slivers of celery for the tails.

Dog Musubi
with SPAM® Hot Dog Rolled Omelet

Rice
1 slice bologna
Nori for eyes, nose, and mouth
Rolled Omelet with SPAM® Hot Dog (see page 78)

Form rice into an oval shape and place into cupcake cup.
From the bologna, cut two tear drop shapes for the ears and a
circle shape for the eye. Tuck ears in between the cupcake cup
and musubi and place circle for the eye on the rice. Finish
with nori eyes, mouth, and nose.

SCRUMPTIOUS
SAMMIES

Sister and Brother Bear Sandwiches

4 slices of your favorite bread
Your favorite deli meat or sandwich filling
2 slices cheddar cheese

1. Cut out the bread and meat with a bear-shaped cutter. Use a small circle cutter to punch holes in the bread for their eyes and a small oval cutter for their noses. Assemble sandwiches.

2. For the bear's clothes for each sandwich, use the bear cutter to cut out the cheddar cheese.

3. With a large circle cutter, cut off the head and feet of the bear shaped cheese. For the girl's shirt use the feet and trim them with the large circle cutter to form the collar of the shirt.

4. Slightly trim the sleeves with a knife and with a small circle cutter make button holes in the shirt. Finally, from the cheese scraps cut out a bow for the girl.

Train Sandwiches

2 slices of your favorite bread
Your favorite deli meat or sandwich filling
1 slice cheddar cheese
1 slice bologna
Mayonnaise for "glue" (optional)

Cut out the bread using a train-shaped cutter. Assemble the
sandwiches using your choice of filling. From the cheddar
cheese, cut out three small squares and one larger square,
then arrange on the train. Then from the
bologna, cut out eight small circles
for the trains wheels and place
on sandwich. Affix cheese and
bologna using the mayonnaise.

Alien Kālua BBQ Pork Sandwich

2 slices cheddar cheese
1 slice mozzarella
   cheese
Small crusty roll
Nori for eyes
3 ounces BBQ Kālua
   Pork (see page 64)
2 decorative picks for
   antennae

Use a large daisy cutter
to cut 1 slice of cheddar
cheese for the inside of the sandwich. Then with the other
slice, cut out two arms and a pair of eyeglasses.

With the mozzarella cheese, cut out the small circle eyes, an
oval nose, and a half moon-shaped mouth.

To assemble, cut the roll in half. On the bottom half place
daisy-shaped cheese, then BBQ Kālua Pork, and top with the
other half of the roll. On top of the roll place the eyeglasses
with the small circle eyes on top of it. Finish eyes with eyes
punched out from nori. Add the nose, mouth, arms, and
antennae.

Keiki Sandwich

2 slices of your favorite bread
Your favorite deli meat or sandwich filling
1 slice mozzarella cheese
1 slice cheddar cheese
1 slice bologna
Nori for eyes

Cut out the bread using a large
circle cutter. Assemble the
sandwich with your choice of
filling. For the keiki's head
use the same large circle cutter to cut the mozzarella, then
cut the hair out of the cheddar
cheese (see picture). From the
bologna, cut out the eyes
with a small circle cutter,
the mouth with a crescent
cutter, and a flower (for
the girl only) with a flower
cutter. For the girl, cut another
smaller flower out of the leftover mozzarella cheese. Assemble the keiki on
the sandwich and finish the eyes with
small circles punched out of the nori.

Butterfly Sandwich

2 slices of your favorite bread
Your favorite deli meat or sandwich filling
1 slice cheddar cheese
1 slice salami
2 sugar eyes
Picks for antennae (optional)

1. Cut the bread out using a
   butterfly-shaped cutter. Assemble
   the sandwich with your choice of
   filling.

2. Cut two ovals out of the cheddar
   cheese to use for the butterfly's
   head and body (see photos).

3. With the circle cutters, cut four
   circles from the salami to decorate
   the wings and a crescent shape for
   the mouth.

4. Add on sugar eyes and finish with
   two decorative picks for the antennae (optional).

Sun-wich

2 slices wheat bread
Your favorite deli meat or sandwich filling
1 slice cheddar cheese
1 slice mozzarella cheese
Nori for eyes and mouth

Cut out the bread using a circle cutter. Assemble the sandwich with your favorite filling. Cut 2 suns out of the cheddar cheese using a sun-shaped cutter and place on the sandwich. Cut 4 small circles for the eyes and a bow (for the girl sun) out of the mozzarella cheese and place on sandwich. Cut 4 large circle eyes out of the nori and punch a small hole in each of the eyes. Punch out a mouth from the nori for each. Finish the sun with the nori eyes and mouth.

Corndog People

3 store-bought mini corndogs
1 slice kamaboko
1 piece of uncooked somen (optional)
Nori for eyes
3 decorative picks (optional)

---

1. Arrange corndogs in container. From kamaboko, cut out eyes and mouths for the corndogs. Fasten with very small pieces of uncooked somen (the somen will be soft from the moisture within two hours). If you don't want to use the somen, just lie the corndogs flat in the bento box.

2. Place nori on eyes and finish corndogs with decorative picks.

Coral Reef Animals
and Tamago with Green Onions

Blue Rice (recipe follows)
A few pieces of wakame, soaked in water for 5 minutes
5 slices of kamaboko
Yellow Color Mist™
Nori
1 hot dog
2 slices of fish sausage
Tamago, with green onions (see page 76)

1. Pack blue rice evenly into the bottom of the container. Place wakame in the corner, on the bottom of the container to look like seaweed.

2. From the kamaboko cut the following: three pieces of coral using a fluted round cutter, one octopus body using a tulip shaped cutter (or you can just use a round cutter), tentacles, two small circles for the octopus eyes, and two large circles for the fish eyes.

3. Spray the octopus body and tentacles with yellow Color Mist™ and let dry for a minute. Assemble the octopus on the rice and finish with

two circles for the eyes and nine small circles for the suckers on the tentacles.

4. Take a hot dog and cut it in half and then cut in half again lengthwise. Cut two notches on the cut end to make the tail. To make the scales, score the hot dog diagonally one way, then go back and score diagonally the other way.

5. Cook hot dog in boiling water or pan fry. Cool hot dog, the kamboko eye, and finish the eye with nori.

6. Lastly, cut star fish from fish sausage and finish with nori for the eyes and mouth.

Blue Rice:
1 cup of washed and drained rice
1 cup of water
5 drops of blue food coloring

Mix everything well together and cook in rice cooker.

Crabs

with Chicken Stir-Fry with Hoisin Sauce and String Beans

Blue Rice (see page 39)
A few pieces of dried wakame, soaked in water for 5 minutes
About 10 slices of kamaboko
Red food coloring
Nori
Stir-Fry (with Chicken and String Beans, see page 72)
Hoisin Sauce (see page 74)

1. Pack Blue Rice evenly into the container. Place the wakame at the ends of the container to look like seaweed.

2. To make coral, cut the kamaboko with a fluted round cutter and a leaf shaped cutter.

3. To make crabs, cut two leaf shapes for the bodies using a round cutter (see photos). Also cut 10 small circles total: for the eyes (four circles), claws (four circles with notches cut into them), and legs (two circles cut in half).

4. Dye all of the crab parts (except for the eyes) in 1 tablespoon of water mixed with 20 drops of red food coloring for a minute. Pull out of dye and dry lightly on a paper towel.

5. Assemble crab on the rice and finish with the eyes and mouths cut from nori.

Hot Dog and Meatball Keiki

1 hot dog
2 Teriyaki Meatballs
   (recipe follows)
Carrot slices, blanched
   and cut into flowers
Nori

Cut the hot dog in half. Slice the cut end (2/3 the length of the hot dog) 3 times, rotate 45 degrees and slice 3 more times to make hair. Cook in boiling water until cooked through. With a small skewer or pick, skewer the meatball, then the carrot, and then the head. Decorate the faces with eyes and mouths cut from nori.

Teriyaki Meatballs
Makes 4 to 6 meatballs

1/2 pound of the Teriyaki Hamburgers recipe (see page 55)
1/2 cup Teriyaki Sauce (see page 55 or use store-bought)

Form teriyaki hamburger into small meatballs and fry until just cooked through. Drain excess oil and add teriyaki sauce and simmer for another 30 seconds and toss so that meatballs are covered with sauce.

Coconuts

with Braised Asian Short Ribs with Maui Onion Sauce

Rice
1 small package katsuobushi (about 1/4 cup)
2 slices kamaboko
2 slices fish sausage
Nori for eyes
Braised Asian Short
    Ribs with Maui
    Onion Sauce (see
    page 56)

Form two balls
with the rice. Roll
in the katsuo-
bushi until well
covered. Cut out
four small circles
for the eyes from the
kamaboko. Cut two small
ovals for the noses from the fish
sausage. Finish eyes with circles cut from nori.

RICE 'N MORE

Doggie Bone SPAM™ Musubi

1 slice SPAM®
Rice
Nori

1. Use a bone-shaped cutter (about the same size as the SPAM® slice) to cut the SPAM®. Pan-fry on both sides.

2. Take a musubi mold and pack rice into it about 3/4 full. Wrap rice with a sheet of nori, then place SPAM® bone on it.

3. To finish, wrap the musubi one more time with another smaller strip of nori.

School Bus SPAM™ Musubi

Rice
1 slice cooked SPAM®
Yellow Color Mist™
1 long 1/2-inch-wide strip of nori
1 slice bologna
1 slice kamaboko

Using a musubi mold fill first with rice, then SPAM®, and then rice again. Carefully spray the top and sides of the musubi with yellow Color Mist™ and let dry.

Wrap the nori strip around the musubi lengthwise (see photo). From the bologna, cut out two circle wheels, four small square windows, and one large square window then assemble on the bus. Cut out "BUS" from the kamaboko using alphabet cutters and place on the bus to finish.

Pumpkin Patch
with Tamago and Fried Chicken Drumettes

Rice
Furikake
3 carrot slices, blanched
2 slices kamaboko
Nori for eyes
Tamago (see
    page 76)
Fried Chicken
    Drumettes
    (see page
    69)

Place rice into the
container. In a small bowl
mix a little rice with furikake.
Using your wet fingers, place the furikake
rice on top of the white rice in the container so that it looks
like the ground of the pumpkin patch (see picture). From the
carrot slices, cut out 3 pumpkins and arrange them on the
rice. From the kamaboko, cut out 8 small circles to use as the
eyes and mouths of the pumpkins. To make the mouth, cut
a circle in half. Cut out a bow for the girl pumpkin from the
pink part of the kamaboko. Arrange the kamaboko on the
pumpkins and finish the eyes with small circles punched out
from the nori.

Fish
with Homemade Chicken Breast Nuggets

Rice
3 jumbo-sized pitted olives
1 slice bologna
1 slice mozzarella
Homemade Chicken Breast Nuggets (see page 68)

---

1. Place rice into a fish-shaped container (or use a fish-shaped cookie cutter to mold rice).

2. Slice the olives crosswise and then in half to form the scales of the fish and place on the rice. Slice an olive lengthwise and place on the rice to form the tail.

3. Out of the bologna, cut a large circle for the eye and two crescent shapes for the mouth and the fin, and place on the fish.

4. To finish the eye, cut a small circle out of the mozzarella for the inner eye, and cut the end off of an olive for the eyeball.

Police Car
and Kabocha with Shiitake Mushrooms and Pork

1 triangle shaped musubi
1 sheet nori
3 slices of fish sausage (or 1 slice bologna)
1 ume
Kabocha with Shiitake Mushrooms and Pork (see page 66)

Wrap the bottom half of the musubi with nori. Cut out three circles from the fish sausage: two for the wheels, and one cut in half and trimmed on the bottom for the cars windows. Place the ume on top of the car the slightly push into the rice to hold.

Piggy
with Chinese-Style Corn Soup

Rice
3 slices fish sausage or 1 slice bologna
Nori for eyes and mouth
Chinese-Style Corn Soup (see page 61)

Pack rice into a circular container. Cut two hearts and an oval from the fish sausage. Use the hearts for the ears. With the oval, take a small circle cutter and punch out two holes for the pig's nose. Cut two circles for the eyes and a small crescent shape for the mouth from the nori.

Two Little Pigs
with Oyako Donburi

Rice
1 slice bologna
Nori for the eyes and mouth
Oyako Donburi (see page 67)

Using a cat or bear-shaped musubi mold, make two small musubis. Cut out four small triangles for the pig's ears and two small ovals for the snout from the bologna. Using a small circle cutter, cut two small holes from each snout for the nose. Finish with nori eyes and mouths.

RECIPES

Hamburgers

Serves 6

2 pounds ground beef
2 eggs
1/2 cup bread crumbs
1/2 cup mayonnaise
1 tablespoon garlic salt
1 teaspoon pepper
2 teaspoons onion powder

Combine all ingredients. Form into patties and cook until cooked through.

Teriyaki Hamburgers

Serves 6

2 pounds ground beef
2 eggs
3 stalks green onion, thinly sliced
1/2 cup bread crumbs
1/2 cup mayonnaise
1 teaspoon pepper
2 teaspoons onion powder
1 tablespoon salt
2 tablespoons or more Teriyaki Sauce for basting (see recipe
    below or use store-bought)

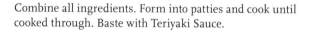

Combine all ingredients. Form into patties and cook until
cooked through. Baste with Teriyaki Sauce.

Teriyaki Sauce

Makes 1 quart

2 cups shoyu
2 cups sugar
1/4 cup mirin
6 stalks green onion, cut into 1-inch pieces
4 (1/4-inch) slices ginger, crushed
4 cloves garlic, crushed

Combine shoyu, sugar, mirin, green onion, ginger, and garlic
in a bowl. Mix well until all the sugar dissolves. Store in the
refrigerator.

Braised Asian Short Ribs

with Maui Onion Sauce

Serves 8

3 to 4 pounds boneless thick-cut short ribs (2-inches thick)
Salt and pepper for seasoning
1 cup flour
Oil
1 extra large Maui onion (or sweet onion), cut in half and
    sliced 1/4-inch
5 cloves garlic crushed
2 thumb-sized 1/4-inch slices of ginger
1-1/2 teaspoons minced lemongrass (use only the tender, bot-
    tom, inner white portion of the lemongrass)
1/2 cup shoyu
1/2 cup packed brown sugar
1 (14.5 ounce) can beef broth
1/2 cup water
1/4 cup sake

Preheat oven to 375 degrees. Cut short ribs in half (or thirds if
it is large), season with salt and pepper, and dust with flour.
In a frying pan, brown short ribs with oil on all sides on
medium high heat. Transfer browned pieces to a large oven-
safe pot with a lid. Drain some of the excess oil from pan
and sauté onions and garlic until onions are soft and start to
caramelize, about 2 to 3 minutes. Transfer cooked onions and
garlic to pot and add in the ginger, lemongrass, shoyu, brown
sugar, beef broth, water, and sake. Bring to a boil on medium

high heat and then cover and place in the oven for 1-1/2 to 2 hours, until the meat is tender. When done, skim the fat from the top and serve as is, or slice the meat and pour the gravy over the top.

Corned Beef Hash

Serves 4

1 russet potato, diced into 1/4-inch cubes
1 can corned beef
1 egg, beaten
2 tablespoons thinly sliced green onions
2 tablespoons minced onion
1/4 teaspoon pepper
Flour
Oil for frying

Cook diced potatoes in boiling water until soft and well cooked. Drain well and cool. Combine the corned beef, egg, green onions, onion, pepper, and cooled potatoes in a large bowl. Form into small patties and lightly dust with flour. Cook in a heated pan with oil until golden and cooked through.

Slow Cooker Kālua Pork

Serves 8 to 10

4- to 5-pound pork
  shoulder
2 tablespoons
  Liquid
  Smoke
2 tablespoons
  Hawaiian
  salt
2 large ti leaves
1 cup water

Rub pork
all over with
Liquid Smoke
and Hawaiian salt,
then wrap in 2 clean ti
leaves. Place pork in slow
cooker, add 1 cup of water to the
bottom of the slow cooker and cover. Cook on high for 5 to 6
hours until the pork is easily shredded. When done, remove
pork from slow cooker, discard ti leaves, and shred pork by
hand or by using two forks. Sprinkle shredded pork with a
little of the cooking liquid to season.

Slow Cooker Okinawan-Style Shoyu Pork

Serves 6

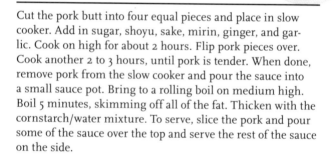

4 pounds boneless pork butt
1 cup sugar
1 cup shoyu
1/4 cup sake
1/4 cup mirin
2 thumb-sized, thin slices of ginger
1 clove garlic, crushed
2 tablespoons cornstarch mixed with 2 tablespoons of water

Cut the pork butt into four equal pieces and place in slow cooker. Add in sugar, shoyu, sake, mirin, ginger, and garlic. Cook on high for about 2 hours. Flip pork pieces over. Cook another 2 to 3 hours, until pork is tender. When done, remove pork from the slow cooker and pour the sauce into a small sauce pot. Bring to a rolling boil on medium high. Boil 5 minutes, skimming off all of the fat. Thicken with the cornstarch/water mixture. To serve, slice the pork and pour some of the sauce over the top and serve the rest of the sauce on the side.

If you can make the pork the day before, it is easier to slice the pork after it has been refrigerated. To reheat the sliced pork you can either microwave or reheat it in a pan with a little chicken broth. Reheat sauce and pour over the top, reserving some on the side.

Chinese-Style Corn Soup

Serves 4 as a starter

1/2 pound of ground
   pork
1 egg white
1 (14.75-ounce) can of
   creamed corn
2 (14-ounce) cans of
   chicken broth
1/2 teaspoon salt
1 pinch of white pep-
   per
1 egg, beaten
1 tablespoon of corn-
   starch mixed with 1
   tablespoon of water

In a bowl, mix ground pork with one egg white. In a pot, place
creamed corn, chicken broth, salt, and white pepper, bring
to a boil on medium high heat. Then add in pork and egg
mixture stirring frequently so that the pork breaks up in the
soup. Bring to a rolling boil and cook for 3 to 5 minutes, until
pork is cooked. Add beaten egg and cornstarch/water mixture
and bring to a boil once more to thicken. Serve with chopped
green onions and cilantro if desired.

Fried Mandoo

Serves 4

1/2 pound ground pork
1/4 pound ground beef
1/2 teaspoon minced garlic
1/2 tablespoon thinly sliced chives
1/2 tablespoon sesame oil
1/2 teaspoon salt
1/4 teaspoon pepper
1 egg, beaten and divided
About 24 mandoo wrappers
Oil for frying

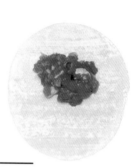

Combine ground pork, ground beef, garlic,
chives, sesame oil, salt, pepper, and 3/4
of the beaten egg in a bowl; mix well.
Place a mandoo wrapper on your
workspace and brush the outside
edges with a little of the remain-
ing beaten egg. In the center of
the wrapper, place 1 tablespoon of
the meat mixture, and fold the wrapper over so that it looks
like a half moon. Crimp the edges of the wrapper to seal.
To cook, heat enough oil to deep-fry the mandoo. Mandoo
is done when the outside is golden and crisp. Serve with
Mandoo Dipping Sauce (recipe follows).

Mandoo Dipping Sauce

1/4 cup shoyu
1/4 cup seasoned Japanese rice vinegar
1 tablespoon thinly sliced green onions
2 teaspoons sesame oil
1 teaspoon toasted sesame seeds

Combine all ingredients and mix well.

BBQ Kālua Pork

Serves 4

2 pounds heated Kālua Pork (see page 59)
3/4 to 1 cup of your favorite barbeque sauce (store-bought)

Drain excess liquid from pork, then toss pork with barbeque sauce. Serve on crusty rolls.

Pan-Fried Pork Chops

Serves 4

4 (6-ounce) pork chops
Garlic salt, pepper,
    and paprika to
    season
1/2 cup flour
    mixed with
    1/2 cup corn-
    starch
Oil for frying

Make small 1/4-
inch cuts on the
edge of the pork
chops (the fatty
edge) to prevent the
pork chop from curling
during cooking. Season
each side of the pork chop
with garlic salt, pepper, and paprika. Dredge each pork chop
through the flour/cornstarch mixture. Shake off excess mixture and pan-fry in heated oil on medium heat until cooked
through.

Kabocha
with Shiitake Mushrooms and Pork

Serves 3

4 ounces ground or
thinly sliced pork
1/4 cup shoyu
1/4 cup sugar
1/8 cup mirin
1 cup water
1/2 teaspoon
dashi no moto
5 large fresh or
rehydrated shii-
take mushrooms
sliced 1/4-inch
1-1/2 pounds of
kabocha, cut into 1- to
1-1/2-inch cubes

In a large sauce pot, combine pork, shoyu, sugar, mirin,
water, and dashi no moto, and cook on medium high until
pork is just cooked. Skim off the fat if there is any. Then
add in kabocha and mushrooms, and bring to a boil. Lower
heat to medium. Let simmer for about 15 minutes, stirring
occasionally (and carefully so that the pumpkin doesn't break
apart) until the pumpkin is cooked through. Be careful not to
overcook, or pumpkin will get mushy.

Oyako Donburi

Serves 4

1 pound chicken, cut
   into small bite-
   sized slices
1/2 of a medi-
   um onion,
   thinly sliced
   into 1/8-
   inch pieces
4 ounces
   mushrooms,
   sliced 1/4-inch
1/4 cup sugar
1/4 cup shoyu
1/2 cup water
2 tablespoons mirin
1/2 teaspoon salt
8 eggs, beaten
Sliced green onions for garnish

In a large sauce pot on medium high, combine the chicken,
onions, mushrooms, sugar, shoyu, water, mirin, and salt,
and cook until chicken is cooked through and onion is soft.
Drizzle in the eggs evenly over the top and cover. Lower heat
to medium low and cook for 5 to 7 minutes until the eggs
have set. Garnish with green onions.

Homemade Chicken Breast Nuggets

Serves 3

1 pound chicken breast
  tenders, cut in half or
  thirds (depending
  on size)
Salt and pepper to
  season
1/2 cup flour
2 eggs, beaten
1 cup bread crumbs
Oil for deep-frying

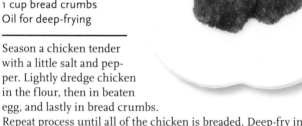

Season a chicken tender
with a little salt and pepper. Lightly dredge chicken
in the flour, then in beaten
egg, and lastly in bread crumbs.
Repeat process until all of the chicken is breaded. Deep-fry in
hot oil until nuggets are cooked through and golden brown.

Fried Chicken Drumettes

Serves 4

2 pounds chicken
  drumettes
1 egg, beaten
½ cup cornstarch
½ cup flour
2 teaspoons gar-
  lic salt
1 teaspoon onion
  powder
1 teaspoon pepper
1 teaspoon salt
Oil for deep frying

Combine chicken with
beaten egg. Then mix
together cornstarch, flour,
garlic salt, onion powder, pep-
per, and salt to make a seasoned flour. Dredge
chicken drumettes in seasoned flour, shake off excess, and
deep-fry until golden and cooked through.

Shrimp Tempura

Serves 4

1-1/2 pounds large shrimp
1 egg
1 cup iced water
1 cup flour
Oil for frying

Clean and devein shrimp, leaving only the tails on. Pat shrimp dry on paper towels. Mix egg, iced water, and flour. Keep the bowl with the batter on ice to keep it chilled. Dip shrimp into batter and deep-fry in preheated oil until golden and cooked through.

Garlic Shrimp Fried Rice

Serves 4

2 tablespoons oil,
   divided
2 eggs beaten
12 ounces shrimp,
   shelled and dev-
   eined
2 cloves garlic, minced
1/2 teaspoon salt
1/4 teaspoon pepper
6 cups day-old cooked
   rice
2 teaspoon shoyu
1 tablespoon oyster sauce
1/2 cup frozen peas
2 tablespoons green onions, thinly sliced

In a non-stick pan on medium heat, scramble eggs with 1/2 teaspoon of oil. Remove eggs and reserve. Add the rest of the oil, shrimp, garlic, salt, and pepper in the pan. Cook until shrimp is almost cooked through. Add in the rice, shoyu, oyster sauce, and peas. Mix and cook until well combined and heated through. Take off heat and stir in green onions and scrambled eggs.

Stir-Fry

Serves 2

Oil
5 ounces protein
4 cups mixed stir-fry vegetables
1/4 cup stir-fry sauce (see recipes on page 74)
1 tablespoon water

In a non-stick wok or large frying pan, heat oil on medium high to high heat. Add protein (except if using tofu, add in last with sauce) and cook until just cooked through. Add in vegetables and cook for a minute. Then add in sauce and water then cook for another minute. Do not overcook; vegetables should still be crisp.

Protein suggestions:
- Beef, pork, or chicken, thinly sliced
- Shrimp, shelled and deveined
- Scallops
- Firm tofu, drained well and cut into bite-sized pieces
- Fish, cut into bite-sized pieces

Suggestions for stir-fry vegetable mix:
- Chinese peas
- Mushrooms halves (if bigger, quarter)
- Carrots, julienned into 1/8-inch pieces
- Celery, sliced into 1/4-inch pieces

- Onions, sliced into 1/4-inch pieces
- Cabbage (won bok or head), cut into 1-1/2-inch pieces
- Bell peppers, sliced 1/4-inch
- Broccoli, 1-inch florets
- Bean sprouts
- Asparagus, cut into 1-1/2-inch pieces
- String beans, cut into 1-1/2-inch pieces

Stir-Fry Sauces

Hoisin Sauce
makes about 3/4 cup

1/2 cup shoyu
1 tablespoon hoisin
1/4 cup sugar
1 clove garlic minced
1 tablespoon dry sherry
1 teaspoon sesame oil
1/4 teaspoon pepper
1-1/2 tablespoons cornstarch

Combine all ingredients and mix well. Mix well again before using for stir-fry.

Chinese Black Bean Sauce

makes about 3/4 cup

1/2 cup shoyu
1/4 cup sugar
2 cloves garlic, minced
1 tablespoon dry sherry
1/2 teaspoon ginger, grated
2 tablespoon oyster sauce
1/4 teaspoon pepper
1 tablespoon Chinese black
   beans, rinsed and
   chopped
1-1/2 tablespoons
   cornstarch

Combine all
ingredients
and mix well.
Mix well again
before using for
stir-fry.

Tamago

Serves 4 as a side

4 eggs
1 tablespoon sugar
1 teaspoon mirin
1 tablespoon water
1/2 teaspoon salt
Non-stick pan spray

Beat together all ingredients except non-stick pan spray.
Heat a tamago egg pan (or a six inch non-stick fry pan) over
medium low heat and spray with non-stick pan spray. Pour
about 1/4 cup of egg mixture into the pan and let cook until
almost set; do not stir. From one end of the pan roll one side
of the egg over about 1 inch and continue to roll egg over until
the end. Spray pan again and pour in another 1/4 cup of egg
mixture. Repeat the process until all of the egg is used. Let
cool slightly before cutting into slices.

Variations:
- To make **SPAM™ Tamago**, add 3 tablespoon chopped
  SPAM® to egg mixture.
- To make **Furikake Tamago**, add 1 tablespoon furikake to
  egg mixture.
- To make **Fish Cake Tamago**, add 2 tablespoons minced
  fish cake to egg mixture.

Soba

Serves 6

1 (12.7-ounce)
   package soba
½ cup soba noo-
   dle soup base
   (store-bought)
   mixed with
1½ cups water
1 cup shredded
   nori
½ cup green onions,
   thinly sliced

Cook soba noodles in boiling water for about 5 minutes.
Drain and run under cold water to cool.
Drain well and serve topped with nori and green onions along
with the soba sauce.

Rolled Omelet

Serves 1

1 egg beaten with 1
teaspoon flour
Item to roll in
the omelete
(cooked hot
dog, SPAM®
hot dog, imi-
tation crab)

Spray a
10-inch frying
pan with non-stick cook-
ing spray. Heat over medium
heat. Pour beaten egg into pan
and cook until just done (don't
stir). With a spatula, carefully flip omelet over and remove
from heat. Take cooked hot dog
(optionally you can use SPAM®
hot dog or imitation crab) and
roll in omelet, see photo. Cut
into bite-sized pieces and skewer
with a pick.

Potato Macaroni Salad

Serves 6 as a side

2 ounces (uncooked weight) elbow macaroni
1 large russet potato, cleaned and cut into 1/2-inch cubes
4 ounces imitation crab, shredded
1/4 cup frozen peas and carrots, thawed
1 hard-boiled egg, cleaned and cut into 1/4-inch pieces
1/2 cup or more mayonnaise
1/4 teaspoon hondashi (Japanese bonito fish soup base)
1/2 teaspoon salt
1/2 teaspoon pepper
1/4 teaspoon sugar

Cook macaroni and potatoes in separate pots until soft, then drain well and cool completely. Add macaroni and potatoes to a large bowl with imitation crab, peas and carrots, egg, mayonnaise, hondashi, salt, pepper, and sugar. Mix well and refrigerate for at least 4 hours. Before serving, mix well and add more mayonnaise if needed.

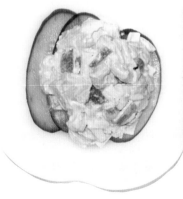

Bento Glossary

Chinese Black Beans:
Fermented black beans used in Chinese cooking

Edamame:
Soybeans

Furikake:
Japanese dried rice seasoning

Hoisin Sauce:
Chinese barbeque dipping sauce

Hondashi:
Japanese bonito fish soup base

Katsuobushi:
Dried shaved bonito flakes

Kamaboko:
Japanese steamed fish cake

Kombu:
Dried Japanese kelp

Mirin:
Japanese sweet rice wine

Musubi:
Japanese rice ball

Nori:
Dried sheets of seaweed

Shoyu:
Japanese term for soy sauce

Soba:
Japanese buckwheat noodles

Somen:
Thin white Japanese wheat-flour noodles

Tamago:
Japanese term for eggs

Wakame:
Mild flavored Japanese seaweed, found usually in dried form

Copyright © 2012 by Mutual Publishing

All rights reserved. No part of this book may be reproduced in any form or by any electronic or mechanical means, including information storage and retrieval devices or systems, without prior written permission from the publisher, except that brief passages may be quoted for reviews.

Library of Congress Control Number: 2012941605

ISBN-10: 1-56647-977-0
ISBN-13: 978-1-56647-977-6

All photos by Susan Yuen unless otherwise indicated as follows.

Dreamstime.com: pg. 13 © Duskbabe, pg. 14 © Mablelo, pg. 19 © Rozum, pg. 22 © Lgrig, pg. 27 © Andrew Kazmierski, pg. 30 © Willeecole, pg. 33 © Arrxxx, pg. 37 © Aniramka33, pg. 40 © Pzaxe, pg. 49 © Epicstock, pg. 53 © Jiri Hera

First Printing, September 2012

Mutual Publishing, LLC
1215 Center Street, Suite 210
Honolulu, Hawai'i 96816
Ph: 808-732-1709
Fax: 808-734-4094
E-mail: info@mutualpublishing.com
www.mutualpublishing.com

Printed in Korea